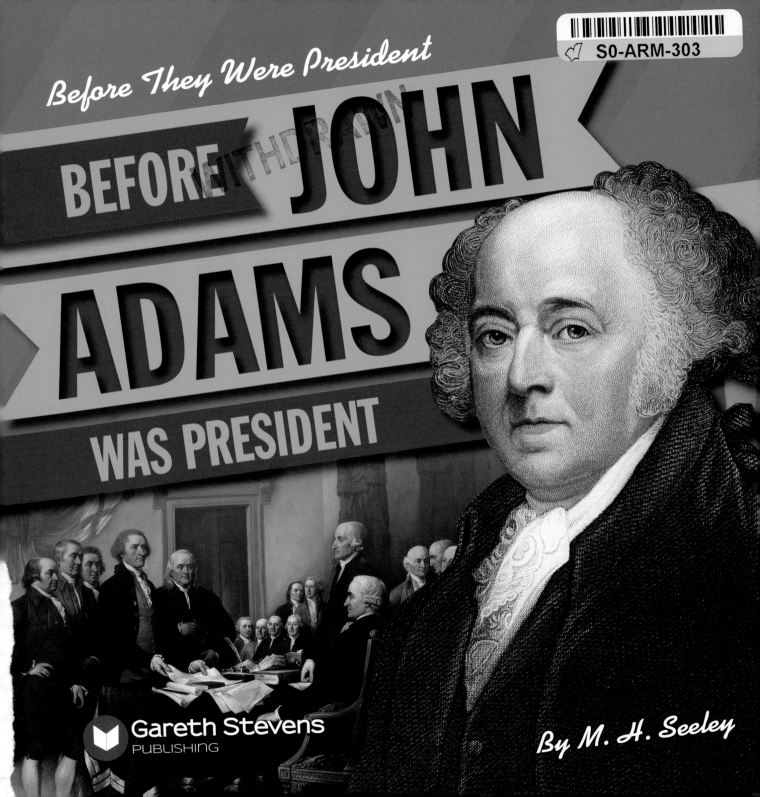

Before They Were President

# BEFORE JOHN ADAMS WAS PRESIDENT

**Gareth Stevens**
PUBLISHING

By M. H. Seeley

Please visit our website, www.garethstevens.com. For a free color catalog of all our high-quality books, call toll free 1-800-542-2595 or fax 1-877-542-2596.

**Cataloging-in-Publication Data**

Names: Seeley, M. H.
Title: Before John Adams was president / M. H. Seeley.
Description: New York : Gareth Stevens Publishing, 2018. | Series: Before they were president | Includes index.
Identifiers: ISBN 9781538210673 (pbk.) | ISBN 9781538210703 (library bound) | ISBN 9781538210680 (6 pack)
Subjects: LCSH: Adams, John, 1735-1826–Juvenile literature.Presidents–United States–Biography–Juvenile literature.
Classification: LCC E322.S4535 2018 | DDC 973.4'4092 B –dc23

First Edition

Published in 2018 by
**Gareth Stevens Publishing**
111 East 14th Street, Suite 349
New York, NY 10003

Copyright © 2018 Gareth Stevens Publishing

Designer: Laura Bowen
Editor: Ryan Nagelhout/Kate Mikoley

Photo credits: Cover, pp. 1 (John Adams), 9 Stock Montage/Archive Photos/Getty Images; cover, p. 1 (background painting) ~riley/Wikimedia Commons; cover, pp. 1–21 (frame) Samran wonglakorn/Shutterstock.com; p. 5 NielsF/Wikimedia Commons; p. 7 Futurist110/Wikimedia Commons; p. 11 Slick-o-bot/Wikimedia Commons; p. 13 Hulton Archive/Getty Images; p. 15 Howcheng/Wikimedia Commons; p. 17 Clindberg/Wikimedia Commons; p 19 (main) bauhaus1000/DigitalVision Vectors/Getty Images; p. 19 (inset) John Hoppner/Wikimedia Commons; p. 21 (John Adams) Everett - Art/Shutterstock.com.

Printed in China

CPSIA compliance information: Batch #CW18GS: For further information contact Gareth Stevens, New York, New York at 1-800-542-2595.

# CONTENTS

Words in the glossary appear in **bold** type the first time they are used in the text.

# THE THINKER

From a young age, the future president John Adams was a person who loved to think. At 15, he was accepted into Harvard College. After finishing college, he began studying law. By 23, he became a **lawyer**.

In the centuries following his presidency, Adams has been remembered less for what he did as president than what he thought about the presidency. Adams had deep **insight** into American **democracy**. His writings are often studied by **political** leaders today.

## Presidential Preview

John Adams's father was a farmer who also worked in a church in the New England town where they lived. He wanted Adams to grow up to work in the church, too.

JOHN ADAMS WAS BORN IN BRAINTREE, NOW KNOWN AS QUINCY, MASSACHUSETTS, IN 1735. THE HOUSE HE WAS BORN IN, SHOWN HERE, IS NOW PART OF A NATIONAL HISTORICAL PARK.

# WORKING ON THE FARM

Adams was the oldest of three children. When he was young, he didn't like school very much and wanted to be a farmer, like his father. Adams's father worried that being a farmer would be a waste of John's cleverness.

One day, John's father took him out into the fields and made him farm for a full day, thinking the hard work would change John's mind. But when he asked John whether he still wanted to be a farmer, John said yes!

## Presidential Preview

Later in his life, Adams wrote that he always wanted to be outside and loved hunting as a young boy.

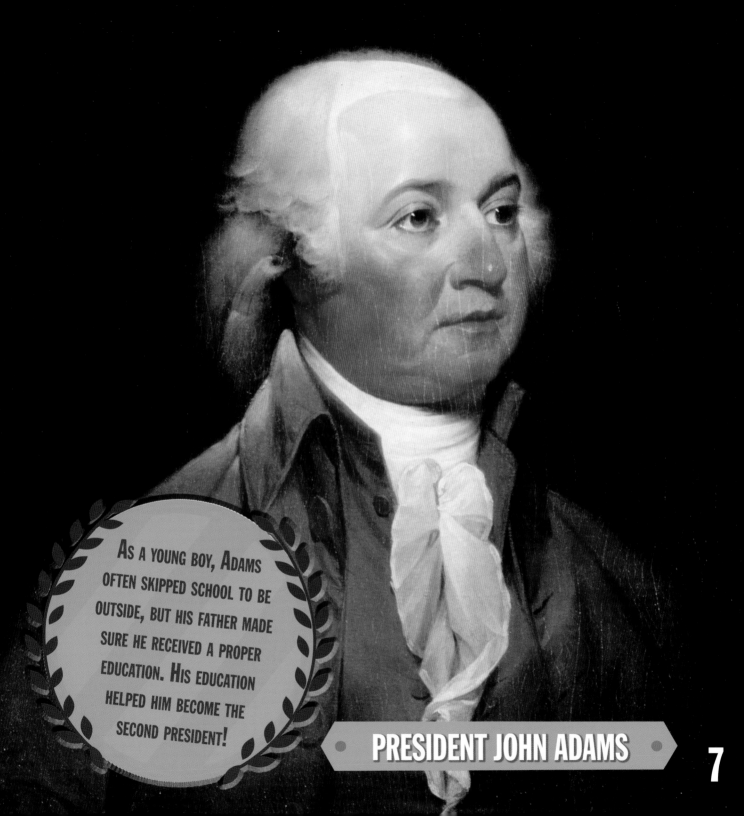

As a young boy, Adams often skipped school to be outside, but his father made sure he received a proper education. His education helped him become the second president!

PRESIDENT JOHN ADAMS

7

# "REMEMBER THE LADIES"

In 1764, Adams married Abigail Smith. John and Abigail's love was so strong that they sent more than 1,100 letters to each other during their lives. Abigail was the person John went to when he needed advice. He trusted her opinion over everyone else's.

Abigail was very smart, and she was a strong voice for women's rights. In one of her most famous letters to John, she wrote, "Remember the ladies ... do not put such unlimited power into the hands of the husbands."

*Presidential Preview*

Within 8 years of being married, John and Abigail had five children. Sadly, one of them, Susanna, died when she was still a baby.

Throughout their life together, Abigail acted as John's unofficial adviser.

9

# LAW AND ORDER

After leaving school, Adams became a lawyer in Boston, Massachusetts. He had only one **client** in his first year and lost the case. But by 1770, Adams had become a very successful lawyer.

In perhaps his most well-known case, Adams **defended** British soldiers who were part of the Boston **Massacre**, a fight in 1770 in which five people were killed. Other Boston lawyers didn't want to defend these British soldiers, but Adams agreed to do it—and he succeeded! None of his clients were sent to jail.

## Presidential Preview

After the **trial** ended, Adams said it was one of the hardest cases he had taken on, but he was very proud that he had.

At the time of the Boston Massacre, the American colonies were still under British rule. It was an important event in the lead-up to the American Revolution, the war that would lead to the independence of the United States.

# MAKE UP YOUR MIND, JOHN ADAMS!

At first, Adams wasn't sure which side he agreed with when it came to the American colonies breaking away from England and forming a new country. He didn't always like the way England ruled the colonies, but he also didn't trust everyone who spoke out in favor of American independence.

As time went on, however, Adams decided that the best way for the colonies to move forward was to become an independent country. By the time the war began, he was an important leader in the movement for independence.

## Presidential Preview

Before the American Revolution, Adams wrote many **essays** and newspaper articles in support of American independence.

SOME OF THE WRITINGS ADAMS HELPED WITH ARE CONSIDERED PROPAGANDA, OR INFORMATION THAT IS OFTEN UNTRUE AND USED TO SUPPORT ONE POINT OF VIEW.

13

# MAKING A STATEMENT

In 1774, Adams became part of the Continental Congress, the governing body of the colonies around the time of the American Revolution. He was chosen to help write the Declaration of Independence, the **document** that said the 13 American colonies were forming their own country.

Adams worked alongside some of the most respected men of his day, including Thomas Jefferson and Benjamin Franklin, to prepare the document. After it was written and agreed upon, 56 men from all 13 colonies signed it.

## Presidential Preview

Adams was one of only two men who signed the Declaration of Independence and later became president. The other was Thomas Jefferson, who was the third president of the United States.

At first, the Congress debated, or argued about, the wording of the Declaration of Independence. Benjamin Franklin, John Adams, and Thomas Jefferson are shown here working on the document.

15

# TREATY OF PARIS

As a member of the Continental Congress, Adams was a busy man. He was part of 90 **committees**—more than any other member of the congress! Adams was often sought out by leaders who wanted to know his thoughts.

In 1779, Adams was chosen to help the colonies come to an agreement for peace with Great Britain. He helped **negotiate** the Treaty of Paris, which ended the American Revolution and officially made the United States its own country. The Treaty of Paris was signed in 1783.

*Presidential Preview*

After the Treaty of Paris was signed in 1783, Adams spent more time in Europe. He arranged other treaties, or agreements, with several countries.

TALKS OF ENDING THE WAR BEGAN BEFORE THE OFFICIAL TREATY OF PARIS WAS SIGNED. ADAMS AND OTHER NEGOTIATORS SIGNED A PRELIMINARY AGREEMENT OF PEACE IN 1782.

17

# CHECKS AND BALANCES

An important part of the American government is that none of the three branches—executive, judicial, or legislative—has too much power. Adams agreed this was important so that no one person or group could rule the rest of the country.

However, Adams also believed that for the country to succeed, it needed a strong president. In 1789, Adams ran to become the first president of the United States. He lost to George Washington, but came in second place. At the time, that meant he would become the vice president.

## Presidential Preview

Adams wrote essays about his belief that the United States needed a strong leader, including a set published in a Philadelphia newspaper.

George III was the king of England when the American colonies declared their independence. Adams's essays made some people think he wanted a king like England had.

KING GEORGE III

JOHN ADAMS

19

# THE SECOND PRESIDENT

In 1797, after serving nearly 8 years as the first US vice president under President George Washington, Adams became the country's second president. He was a Federalist, which was a political group that believed in a strong national government.

Adams was president for 4 years, but lost to Thomas Jefferson in the election of 1800. After he was done leading the nation, he spent much of his time writing about his life and thoughts. In 1825, his son, John Quincy Adams, became the sixth president of the United States.

## Presidential Preview

John Adams died on July 4, 1826—exactly 50 years after the Declaration of Independence was approved. He died the same day as Thomas Jefferson.

# The Life of John Adams

**1735** — Adams is born in Braintree, Massachusetts.

**1755** — Adams finishes Harvard College.

**1756** — Adams begins studying law with a lawyer in Massachusetts.

**1758** — Adams begins practicing law in Boston, Massachusetts.

**1764** — Adams marries Abigail Smith.

**1770** — The Boston Massacre takes place in March. Adams defends the British soldiers who were charged for the Boston Massacre.

**1774** — Adams becomes part of the First Continental Congress.

**1776** — Adams helps write the Declaration of Independence, which is approved on July 4.

**1783** — The Treaty of Paris is signed.

**1789** — Adams becomes the first vice president of the United States

**1797** — Adams becomes the second president of the United States.

PRESIDENT JOHN ADAMS

JOHN ADAMS PLAYED A BIG PART IN AMERICAN HISTORY, EVEN BEFORE HE BECAME PRESIDENT!

# GLOSSARY

**client:** a person who pays somebody else to help them do something

**committee:** a group of people who are chosen to do a certain job together

**defend:** to keep someone or something safe. Also, to work for someone who is being charged with a crime.

**democracy:** a system of government in which people vote for their leaders

**document:** a formal piece of writing

**essay:** a piece of writing

**insight:** an understanding of a situation or problem

**lawyer:** someone whose job it is to help people with their questions and problems with the law

**massacre:** the killing of a large number of people

**negotiate:** to come to an agreement

**political:** having to do with the activities of the government and government officials

**preliminary:** coming before the main part of something

**trial:** the court process of figuring out whether or not someone committed a crime

# FOR MORE INFORMATION

## Books

Gould, Jane H. *John Adams.* New York, NY: PowerKids Press, 2013.

Gregory, Josh. *John Adams: The 2nd President.* New York, NY: Bearport Publishing, 2015.

## Websites

**Biography: President John Adams**
*www.ducksters.com/biography/uspresidents/johnadams.php*
Learn more about the life and presidency of John Adams here.

**John Adams**
*www.american-historama.org/presidents-united-states/john-adams.htm*
Watch a video about John Adams's life and read about his presidency.

**John Adams**
*www.whitehouse.gov/1600/presidents/johnadams*
Read about John Adams's life story on the official White House website.

# INDEX